Kids in the Kitchen™
The Library of Multicultural Cooking

FOOD AND RECIPES OF AFRICA

Theresa M. Beatty

The Rosen Publishing Group's
PowerKids Press™
New York

The recipes in this book are intended for a child to make together with an adult.
Many thanks to Ruth Rosen and her test kitchen.

Published in 1999 by The Rosen Publishing Group, Inc.
29 East 21st Street, New York, NY 10010

First Edition

Book Design: Resa Listort

Photo Illustrations: Cover photo by John Bentham; p. 7 © Sean Morris; p. 8 © Eric L. Wheater; pp. 10, 12, 18 © Ira Fox; p. 14 © John Novajosky; pp. 11, 13, 15, 19 © Pablo Maldonado; p. 16 © Travelpix/FPG International; p. 20 © Jean Kugler/FPG International.

Beatty, Theresa M.
    Food and recipes of Africa / by Theresa M. Beatty.
        p.   cm. — (Kids in the kitchen : multicultural cooking)
    Includes index.
    Summary: Describes some of the foods enjoyed in the different regions of Africa and provides recipes for dishes popular in these areas.
    ISBN 0-8239-5220-7
    1. Cookery, African—Juvenile literature. 2. Food habits—Africa—Juvenile literature. [1. Food habits—Africa.
    2. Cookery—African.] I. Title. II. Series: Beatty, Theresa M. Kids in the kitchen.
TX725.A3B43 1998
641.596—dc21   98-11215
                                                                                                          CIP
                                                                                                          AC

Manufactured in the United States of America

CONTENTS

Abbreviations: cup = c.   tablespoon = tbsp.   teaspoon = tsp.
liter = l   milliliter = ml

AFRICA

The huge **continent** (KON-tih-nent) of Africa is home to more than 45 countries and many different **cultures** (KUL-cherz). Africa's **landscapes** (LAND-skayps) are made up of deserts, grasslands, mountains, and beautiful forests.

Because of these different landscapes, certain types of food that are common in one part of Africa may not be found in another. This is why Africa has so many different cooking styles.

Close neighbors of Africa, like the peoples of the Middle East, also added to the foods and cooking styles of Africa. And when Europeans came to Africa, they too brought many of their cooking styles with them.

◀ *More than one billion people live on the continent of Africa.*

AFRICAN COOKING STYLES

African cooking uses the freshest foods. If one fresh vegetable is out of season, another is used in its place.

Africans don't usually follow recipes as strictly as we do. Instead, people learn the basics of recipes by listening to their elders. Then they build on the older recipes by adding new ingredients or changing the amounts of certain ingredients used. This cooking style makes African food an adventure!

When Africans eat meat, they use it only to flavor dishes. Meat is usually not a main **course** (KORS). Instead, it is cooked in tasty soups or stews with vegetables, spices, and other delicious ingredients.

Africans often grind their own flour and spices. ▶

AFRICAN HOSPITALITY

Many cultures in Africa are known for their great **hospitality** (HOS-pih-TA-luh-tee). And food is a very important part of this hospitality. Africans use food as a way of welcoming people into their homes and making their guests feel comfortable.

In many parts of Africa, guests are offered a delicious meal as soon as they arrive at someone's home. As a sign of respect for their host or hostess, guests always eat a few bites of the food that is offered to them, even if they are not very hungry.

Meals bring friends and families together in Africa, as they do in most countries throughout the world.

FOODS OF AFRICA

People who live along the coast of West Africa, in countries like Senegal and Liberia, eat lots of fish because they are so close to the Atlantic Ocean. People living in countries in the eastern part of Africa, such as Ethiopia and Tanzania, eat more meat than other Africans because they have more cattle there.

The foods and cooking styles are different all over Africa, but there are some things that almost all Africans eat. Vegetables and fruits like **cassava** (kuh-SAH-vuh), bananas, yams, **plantains** (PLAN-tunz), beans, and lentils are eaten in all parts of Africa. Peanuts, called ground nuts in Africa, are popular too.

DOVI
(WEST AFRICAN PEANUT BUTTER STEW)

YOU WILL NEED:

2 tbsp. *(30 ml)* butter
2 medium onions
2 garlic cloves,
   minced
1 tsp. *(5 ml)* salt
½ tsp. *(2 ml)* black
   pepper
1 chili pepper, with
   seeds removed,
   minced
1 chicken, cut into
   serving pieces
2 green bell peppers,
   with seeds and core
   removed, chopped
3–4 tomatoes,
   chopped
2 c. *(500 ml)* water
3 tbsp. *(40 ml)* smooth
   peanut butter

HOW TO DO IT:

▲ Melt butter in a large stew pot over medium heat.
▲ Add onions. Brown until golden.
▲ Add garlic, salt, black pepper, and chili pepper.
▲ Cook for 2 to 3 minutes, stirring all the time.
▲ Add chicken pieces and bell peppers.
▲ Continue cooking, stirring every few minutes, until chicken is browned on all sides.
▲ In a bowl, mash tomatoes with a fork.
▲ Stir in the tomatoes and the water.
▲ Reduce heat to low and simmer for 10 minutes.
▲ In another bowl, mix the peanut butter with a little bit of broth from the pot.
▲ Stir in the peanut butter mixture.
▲ Simmer for 1 to 1½ hours, or until chicken is well done.

Serves 4–6

Always ask a grown-up to help you when using knives!
Always ask a grown-up to help you when using the stove or oven!

FOODS OF WEST AFRICA

West Africa includes countries such as Ghana, Mali, Nigeria, and Sierra Leone. Most West African countries lie along the Atlantic Ocean. Many people who live in these countries are fishermen and fisherwomen.

In addition to fish, rice is another **staple** (STAY-pul), or main part, of the West African diet. The weather is rainy in countries like Liberia, so rice grows very well there. Spicy stews and soups are popular dishes.

The **climate** (KLY-mit) in West Africa is perfect for growing many **tropical** (TRAH-pih-kul) fruits like bananas, coconuts, grapefruit, guavas, mangoes, and pineapples.

WEST AFRICAN COCONUT SOUP

YOU WILL NEED:

6 c. *(1.5 l)* beef broth

1½ c. *(375 ml)* firmly
   packed coconut
   flakes

1 eggplant, peeled
   and diced

1 tbsp. *(15 ml)* lemon
   juice

½ tsp. *(2 ml)* salt

¼ tsp. *(1 ml)* ground
   ginger

chopped parsley

HOW TO DO IT:

▲ Combine broth and coconut in large pan and bring to a boil.
▲ Add eggplant, lemon juice, salt, and ginger.
▲ Cover, reduce heat, and simmer for 30 minutes.
▲ Remove from heat and cool.
▲ Mix soup in a blender for 30 seconds.
▲ Return to pan and heat well.
▲ Serve topped with parsley.

Serves 6

Always ask a grown-up to help you when using knives!
Always ask a grown-up to help you when using the stove or oven!

FOODS OF EAST AFRICA

East African countries include Ethiopia, Tanzania, and Kenya. A typical East African meal consists of a stew with meat such as goat, beef, or **mutton** (MUH-tun), and a **starch** (STARCH) like rice, potatoes, or plantains.

A thin pancake-like bread called *injera* (in-JAYR-ah) is popular with Ethiopians. For traditional meals, the cook makes the bread and then drapes it like a tablecloth over a large pan or tray.

Then, the cook places tasty stews and sauces right on the bread in little piles. Instead of using forks and spoons, dinner guests pull off small sections of the bread and use it to scoop up the food. By the end of the meal, the food and all the bread are eaten!

14

PLANTAIN AND VEGETABLE SALAD

Plantains look like big bananas and are popular all over Africa. Unlike bananas, they don't taste good raw. However, they are very tasty when cooked. You can buy plantains in many food stores throughout the world.

YOU WILL NEED:

3 large unripe (green) plantains or green bananas

water for boiling the plantains

¼ tsp. (1 ml) salt

1 red onion, thinly sliced

1 tomato, diced

1 c. (250 ml) washed, chopped fresh spinach

2 tbsp. (30 ml) chopped fresh cilantro or ½ tsp. (2 ml) dried cilantro

¼ tsp. (1 ml) black pepper

3 tbsp. (40 ml) olive oil

2 tbsp. (30 ml) red wine vinegar

HOW TO DO IT:

▲ Peel plantains and cut into bite-sized pieces.
▲ Place pieces in a pot and add enough water to cover them.
▲ Add salt and place pot on stove over high heat.
▲ Bring to a boil.
▲ Reduce heat and simmer over low flame for 10 to 15 minutes, or until plantains are soft (use a fork to test them).
▲ Remove pot from heat.
▲ Drain water from pot and place plantain pieces in a large serving bowl.
▲ Add onions, tomato, spinach, cilantro, and pepper.
▲ Pour in oil and vinegar.
▲ Toss until all ingredients are mixed well.

Serves 4–6

Always ask a grown-up to help you when using knives!
Always ask a grown-up to help you when using the stove or oven!

15

SHARING CULTURES

Throughout history, people have traveled to different places. And when people visit distant lands, they discover new ways of living. They also share their own ways of living with the new people they meet. This includes foods and styles of cooking.

This is what happened in Africa. The countries of the Middle East are very close to the eastern and northern parts of Africa. For centuries, people have traveled back and forth between these two areas, bringing their foods with them. That's how food and spices from the Middle East, such as saffron, ended up in African recipes.

◀ *Morocco shares languages as well as styles of cooking with Europe. In addition to the languages of Arabic and Berber, many Moroccans also speak French and Spanish.*

17

FOODS OF NORTH AFRICA

The countries of Morocco and Algeria are in North Africa. These countries and others in the area are very close to Europe. In fact, one part of Morocco is only eight miles from Spain!

Morocco, like other countries in northwestern Africa, shares part of its culture with Europe and the Middle East. People from France, Italy, and Spain have all **settled** (SEH-tuld) in northwestern Africa in the past. Arabs have lived there since the 7th century. Moroccans learned to use spices such as marjoram and cumin from Arab cultures.

One popular Moroccan dish is **couscous** (KOOS-koos). Couscous is a semolina dish that is often served with lamb, chicken, or beef.

MOROCCAN COUSCOUS

YOU WILL NEED:

2 tbsp. *(30 ml)* peanut
  or vegetable oil
1 c. *(250 ml)* chopped
  onions
2 tomatoes, finely
  chopped
1 clove garlic, crushed
1 c. *(250 ml)* couscous
1 tsp. *(5 ml)* powdered
  coriander
½ tsp. *(2 ml)* salt
1 tsp. *(5 ml)* crushed
  red pepper
½ tsp. *(2 ml)* saffron
1 tsp. *(5 ml)*
  powdered cumin
1 tsp. *(5 ml)* curry
  powder
1 c. *(250 ml)* canned
  chickpeas
1 c. *(250 ml)* water

HOW TO DO IT:

▲ Place oil in a large skillet over medium heat.
▲ Add onions, tomatoes, and garlic.
▲ Stir often for about 5 minutes.
▲ Remove from heat and cover.
▲ Place couscous, coriander, salt, red pepper, saffron, cumin, curry powder, and chickpeas in a medium pot.
▲ In a separate pot, boil the water and add to the couscous mixture.
▲ Cover and let stand for 5 minutes.
▲ In a large bowl, combine the couscous mixture with the vegetable mixture.
▲ Fluff with a fork and serve.

Serves 4

Always ask a grown-up to help you when using knives!
Always ask a grown-up to help you when using the stove or oven!

19

THE SPREAD OF AFRICAN FOOD

When people move to different places, they bring part of their culture with them. Through **relocation** (ree-loh-KAY-shun) and trade, Africans have brought their foods and cooking styles to different countries all over the world.

Africans were cruelly taken from Africa in the 1700s and 1800s. They were brought to North America, South America, and islands in the Caribbean and turned into **slaves** (SLAYVZ) for **plantation** (plan-TAY-shun) owners. Some of these Africans brought the seeds of certain foods with them. Since slaves did most of the cooking on the plantations, African tastes and foods quickly became part of American cooking. The horrible practice of slavery finally ended in the late 1800s.

◀ *People, such as these Moroccan men, still travel great distances on mules and camels and share their cultures and cooking styles with people of other lands.*

AFRICAN FOOD IN THE UNITED STATES

Louisiana's famous Cajun and Creole cooking styles are based in part on African food. Okra is often used in these kinds of cooking. Soul food, a **cuisine** (kwih-ZEEN) created by African Americans, also uses ingredients from Africa, such as black-eyed peas.

The next time you eat a peanut-butter-and-jelly sandwich, think of Africa. It was Africans who brought peanuts, or ground nuts, to the United States and made them so popular.

When you prepare some of the delicious recipes here, share them with family and friends because this is the African **tradition** (truh-DIH-shun).

GLOSSARY

cassava (kuh-SAH-vuh) A starchy vegetable that is kind of like a potato.

climate (KLY-mit) The weather conditions of a certain place.

continent (KON-tih-nent) A very large area of land.

course (KORS) One of a number of dishes that make up a whole meal.

couscous (KOOS-koos) A Middle Eastern grain often used in cooking.

cuisine (kwih-ZEEN) A style of cooking.

culture (KUL-cher) The beliefs, customs, art, and religion of a group of people.

hospitality (HOS-pih-TA-luh-tee) The friendly treatment of guests.

injera (in-JAYR-ah) A pancake-like bread that is popular in Ethiopia.

landscape (LAND-skayp) The landforms in a certain part of a country.

mutton (MUH-tun) The meat of a sheep.

plantain (PLAN-tun) A banana-like fruit.

plantation (plan-TAY-shun) A large farm on which crops such as cotton, tobacco, sugarcane, and rubber trees are grown.

relocation (ree-loh-KAY-shun) Moving to a new place.

settle (SEH-tul) To set up a home or a colony in another country.

slave (SLAYV) A person who is "owned" by another person and is forced to work for him.

staple (STAY-pul) A very important and basic food item.

starch (STARCH) A group of foods that includes bread, pasta, and rice.

tradition (truh-DIH-shun) A way of doing something that is passed down through a family.

tropical (TRAH-pih-kul) From an area that is very hot and humid.

23

INDEX